THE STORY OF
BOLTON CASTLE

An introduction to the Wensleydale
fortress of the Scropes

BY

George Jackson

With drawings by

Fred Lawson

The Castle from the West

Dalesman Books
1980

The Dalesman Publishing Company Ltd.,
Clapham (via Lancaster), North Yorkshire.

First published 1956

Tenth impression 1980

© George Jackson, 1956, 1980

ISBN: 085206 087 4

Printed by Galava Printing Company Limited, Nelson, Lancashire

The Castle from the North-East

1 - Building of the Castle

STANDING on the northern slopes of Wensleydale, Bolton Castle was built by Richard, the first Lord Scrope, during the last quarter of the 14th century. On the accession of Richard II, Lord Scrope was appointed Steward of the Royal Household and later to the Chancellorship of England. While holding this office he sought and obtained the Royal Licence to crenellate his manor house at Bolton. The licence appears to be a formal sanction for building operations, which at that date 4th July, 1379, were already well in hand, for a building contract of the year before (14th September, 1378) for a portion of the southern range, suggests by its terms that these parts were a continuation of work already erected in northern and western sections of the building.

The building contract, between Sir Richard le Scrope and John Lewyn, mason, made provision for a "tower for a kitchen, a gatehouse and other buildings to be vaulted and embattled. The towers were to be fifty feet in height below the battlements and the other buildings forty feet in height below the battlements." For the most part these measurements were adhered to, the only exception being the towers, which rise to almost one hundred feet as compared with the stipulated fifty.

The cost of "crenellating the manor house" amounted to 1,000 marks per annum and occupied a period of eighteen years, during which time the subject of the terms—the manor house—appears to have entirely disappeared!

Though designed as a fortress the function of the Castle from the very beginning appears to have been residential rather than military. In plan it follows a pattern which developed during the 14th century

—a rectangular curtain built round a courtyard, with a strong tower at each corner and a smaller turret in the centre of each curtain. At Bolton, these smaller turrets appear on the north and south sides only, an arrangement which suggests a last minute change of plans, for the original contract stipulates that the gatehouse should be built in a separate tower in the east curtain.

The position of the Castle, which Leland describes as "in a roke side," is not strategically strong. The high ground to the north exposes the watch towers and courtyards to projectiles of all kinds, while the fall of ground to the south does away with all possibilities of a moat. But the structure, as present-day masons agree, is superbly built, and a local tradition attributes its stability to the mixing of the mortar with ox blood.

Stone for building was plentiful and near at hand, that for general purposes being obtained from a quarry immediately behind the village, whilst freestone for quoins, arches and finer details came from Greets Quarry on the moors, three miles to the north of Bolton. Timber presented a greater problem. Because the oaks of Wensleydale were stunted and lacking in length and straightness for the chamber spans at Bolton it was necessary to seek them further afield. Leland, in his *Itinerary*, tells us that "most parte of the tymber that was occupied in buyldynge of this castell was gett out of the forest of Engleby, in Cumberland, and Richard, Lord Scrope for covenaunce of it had layde by the was dyvers drawghts of oxen to cary it from place to place till it came to Bolton."

The most casual visitor to Bolton cannot fail to be impressed, and to some extent bewildered, by the maze of rooms, passages and stairs which appear to have been built at random and without thought for use or convenience. With greater familiarity, however, the building reveals the skill and ingenuity with which the whole has been planned to hinder and confound any adversary seeking to take unlawful possession. Any forces who succeeded in gaining a part of the ground floor would still be at a loss to find direct approaches to other sections and the upper regions. Another point of interest in the defence planning is the construction of the spiral staircases. These, with only one or two exceptions (for which there may be a reason not now apparent) are built so as to turn right as they ascend, an arrangement which provides a maximum space for the sword arm, thus giving great advantage to those defending from above.

When as early as the 12th century it had been proved a serious disadvantage in case of siege for castles to be unprovided with alternative means of supply and escape, it seems strange that a man as experienced in war as Richard Scrope should plan his fortress with only one entrance. Yet such is the case at Bolton, where the gatehouse in the east curtain was originally the sole means of entry and exit. Today there are two additional entrances, one on the north side and the other on the west, but these are modern and had no part in the original plan.

Gatehouse showing Porter's Lodge

2 - Tour of the Castle

The Gatehouse This consists of a vaulted passage originally defended at each end by a portcullis. The archway at the courtyard end is open, but the one leading from outside is rebated to carry a heavy two-leaved door. The stonework of the rebate is much mutilated where the hinge-crooks have been broken away. The lock from the door is still preserved in the Castle Museum. The floor is paved with flags and there are indications that a stone bench ran along the wall at each side.

The Porter's Lodge On the left, just inside the gatehouse, a low doorway leads into the porter's lodge, a vaulted cell built into the corner of the south-east tower. The cell was warmed by a small fireplace with a chimney that ascends to the top of the tower. The lodge was originally lit by two small unglazed slits, provided with oak shutters to protect the porter from the weather and enemy missiles. One window looks eastward down the village and the other faces north to enable the occupant to scrutinize all who stood on the Castle threshold seeking admission.

The   Although an interesting medieval defence, the portcullis
Portcullis at its best seems but a clumsy contrivance. The raising
and lowering of heavy grills in stone grooves suggests
the possibility of serious jams, particularly when (as at Bolton) the
grills were suspended by a single chain. All the grills—there were
seven—have disappeared, so that particulars of their design and
contruction are lacking. The grooves of the gatehouse grills are
square throughout, but those of the smaller grills in the courtyard
are semi-circular in the lower half, indicating that the sides of the
grills were rounded.

The   A sensation of awe may, or may not, have been a motive
Courtyard in the minds of the designers when they planned the
inner approach to the Castle, but it is certain that those
entering for the first time could not fail to be impressed (or oppressed,
according to the circumstances of their visit) when they arrived in
the courtyard, for the surrounding walls are so lofty that the propor-
tions of this large area are contracted to the semblance of a sunless
pit.

Five doors open from the courtyard into various parts of the
Castle interior, doors so inconspicuously placed that a person riding
hurriedly into the courtyard could be momentarily under the impression that further means of entry did not exist. With the eventual
discovery that there were five doors to select from it would still be
impossible to single out any particular entry as the principal one.
These arrangements were obviously intentional, for an ememy force,
having succeeded in forcing the gatehouse, might still meet with
disaster whilst hesitating in uncertainty in the courtyard. A glance
up at the towers will show how each of the four corner doors was
defended by a machicolation.

The tall, cinque-foil headed windows in the north wall are those
of the Great Hall, and those in the south wall lit the chapel. A
depression in the ground at the north-east corner of the court marks
the site of the horse trough which was supplied with water, via a
stone spouting, from the well-chamber within the north curtain. The
trough still functions on the green at the east end of the village. It
was moved there at some unknown date after the Castle's dismantling

The South-East The door on the left as one enters from the gate-
Tower   house opens into the entrance of the south-east
tower, which is just a shell, the roof and all the
floors being absent. It is known as the Garrison Tower, for in its
original state the ground-floor room, which had a barrel-vaulted roof
and flagged floor, would serve as the guard room. This is the only
ground-floor room of the three remaining towers to be provided
with a fireplace.

The first-floor room above served as a mess room, a nearby room
on the same floor in the south curtain being the mess kitchen. The

second-floor room above may have been reserved for officers. That this was a room of some importance seems proved by the insertion of a mullion and transom window on the south side sometime during the early 16th century, and also by the fact that a piece of elaborate plaster moulding can still be seen on the north wall just below the fireplace of the room above.

The Courtyard

The two top floors were probably used for sleeping quarters. While in this tower visitors should note the stone light brackets, the curious two-way opening above the east window of the mess-room and widely-splayed window embrasure of the top floor east window.

The Secret Chamber What remains of this interesting room can be seen from the entrance passage leading into the guard room.

There have been three small rooms of similar dimensions to the ground-floor passage, one above the other. The middle one was, in its original condition, vaulted and very low, with a small window in the south wall but no entrance doorway. The only means of entry was by a trap door from the room above. Three sides of this trap can be seen in the remains of the vaulting at the north end.

The South   The whole of the ground floor of the south curtain
Curtain   appears to have been devoted to baking and brewing.
The first chamber, as one enters from the guard room
end, was probably the kneading-house, the second chamber (in which
can be seen the beds of two ovens) being the meal house. Arched
recesses on the east and north walls would accommodate wooden
flour and meal bins. The third chamber was the bakehouse and brew-
house combined, and the entrance to the bread ovens was in the
east wall. Between the two arches and the single one is a wide flue to
carry away the smoke from the thorn fires, in the heat-retaining ashes
of which the loaves were baked. A similar arrangement, now built up,
supplied heat for the brewing vat, the remains of which can be seen
from the stairs leading from the south-west tower to the courtyard.

The   This is the first floor room immediately above the
Mess-Kitchen   kneading house. Its chief interest lies in two fireplaces in the west wall. These are now partially
destroyed, but the fact that there were two in a comparatively small
chamber suggests that their function was not solely that of heating.
The stones of each are burnt, proving their extensive use in times
when it was the custom to roast flesh before open fires. Two windows
in the south wall are constructed at different levels, an arrangement
which has a confusing effect when this part of the building is viewed
from outside. This must have been a deliberate plan to divert
attention from the nearby window of the secret room.

The Auditor's   This room lies immediately above the mess-kitchen.
Chamber   Its purpose, as the place where all the business of
the Castle and estates would be transacted, is sug-
gested by its nearness to the secret chamber, access to which was

The Malting House

Chapel looking East

possible only from the small room off the east end of the chamber.
The importance of the room is further emphasised by the insertion
of a 16th century mullion and transom window in the south wall.

Malthouse   The western end of the first floor in the south curtain
and Granary   is more or less intact. There are two chambers with
               vaulted roofs and chutes in the floors to the bake-
house below. The chambers appear to have been used originally as
granary and malthouse respectively.

Recently the eastern room has been arranged as a 19th century
farm kitchen with furnishings, crockery and utensils of the period
collected over many years by Mrs. J. R. Hopper, of Askrigg—
whose inspiration the kitchen was—and her committee consisting
of Mr. T. C. Calvert, Geroge Jackson and Mr. James Peacock.
Arrangements for this unique display were made with the gracious
permission of Lord Bolton and the tableau, known as The Wensleydale Kitchen, was formally opened on April 10th, 1965, by Lady
Bolton.

The   The Chapel was dedicated to St. Anne in 1399, and en-
Chapel   dowed by the founder as a chantry for six priests to say
               daily masses for the repose of the soul Richard II. In the
east wall is a piscina, and in the turret on the south side are three
cells, the two lower ones being entered from the chapel. The upper
one is reached from a walk which passed behind the now destroyed
battlements of the roof. Each cell has a fireplace and lavatory, and in
the middle cell there is a squint looking on to the position of the
altar, of which no trace remains.

In the corresponding turret on the north side of the Castle are
three similar cells, and it has been suggested that the cells were provided for the six priests attached to Chantry chapel. The tall windows
in the north and south sides of the Chapel have cinque-foil heads
and transoms, which agrees with the contemporary—Perpendicular
—style. The masonry of the windows shows grooves for the insertion of glass, a feature not universal throughout the building.

At the west end of the Chapel a wide semi-circular arch forms a
deep alcove, over which is a plaftorm described as "The Lady's
Gallery." The gallery, which originally had a front wall and possibly
a grill looking into the Chapel, is entered via a narrow staircase from
the south-west tower. In a turret on the same tower hung the Chapel
bell, rung from a cell near the Chapel door.

From the details of the will of Richard, the first Lord Scope, dated
2nd August, 1400 (*Testamenta Eboracensia*) we know that the
Chapel was richly endowed with vestments and altar furnishings.
Extracts from the will read as follows:- "To John, Abbot of the
Monastery of St. Agatha, Easby, my best censor, best chalice, two
best gold candlesticks, two gold cruets and one bell made of gold,
and one cup with cover, which I had as a gift from the Domini
Principis." The Abbot also was to receive "my best vestment with
all appertaining to it, with alb, almeta and embroidered stole."

To his son Roger he left "for use in the Chapel in the Castle at
Bolton, my second best complete vestment," together with "my best
spiceplate, and my second missal, with my porteus which I used at
the saying of matins and vespers." To Roger also was bequeathed
"a pair of paternosters of coral, which once belonged to the Lord my
father, and a gold cross which I used and bore with the blessing of
Almighty God, of the most glorious Virgin Mary, the blessed St.
Anne and all the Saints and me."

The South-West   Of the three remaining towers (originally there
Tower   were four; one at each corner of the building),
                     that at the south-west angle alone remains more
or less intact. It is difficult to say why the rooms in this tower and
those of the west curtain evaded the order of the Commonwealth
Committee of York which decreed that the Castle should be rendered
untenable. It is possible the owners were allowed to retain this rem-
nant until alternative accommodation was found. Bolton Hall, where

the family eventually settled, was built thirty years later. But whatever the reason, it was a fortunate chance which has enabled succeeding generations to see a portion of the Castle in a state little altered from the original.

South-West Tower
Ground Floor   Few people entering this room for the first time fail to be impressed by its massive walls and heavy vaulting, features which demonstrate perhaps more than anywhere else in the building, the Castle's strength and stability.

The
Horse Mill   The widely-splayed south window and the one to the west together with the concaved easement in the north wall, suggest that the west end of this chamber was designed to house a horse mill—two millstones in the centre, with a shaft attached to the upper one, to which a horse was yoked to provide motive power. The floor has mostly been re-laid, but part of the original circular paving still remains near the entrance. The eastern end of the chamber may have been used as a threshing floor. A door in the north wall of this chamber leads into the armourer's forge.

Armourer's
Forge   This chamber is dimly lit today because the modern steps of the west entrance to the Castle are built across the window which provided the chief source of light. A forge stood in the east wall. Originally it had a stone fender, remains of which can still be seen, at a convenient working height from the floor. The present floor, which is at a higher level than the original floor, probably dates from the 18th century when this and other ground floor chambers were used as stables. In the south wall are two deep recesses for the smith's tools. The first smith to be in charge of this forge must have been the one remembered in Lord Scrope's will:—"Item, to Alexander the iron-worker 5 marks."

South-West
Tower   The first-floor room of this tower is now used as part of the restaurant which occupies most of the west curtain of this floor. The original plan of this part of the building is difficult to follow because of the modern partition walls with which it is divided. The west entrance (also modern) by which the visitor enters the castle, opens into this part of the building.

"Mary's Room"   During the 19th century it was felt that visitors would wish to have Mary of Scotland's apartments pointed out. It was therefore decided indiscriminately to show the second-floor room of this tower as "Mary's Room." It is more than doubtful, however, that Mary ever occupied this room during her imprisonment here in 1568-69. The state apartments of the Castle were situated in the north-west tower, and since, whilst at

Bolton, Mary was allowed to retain her royal status it seems reasonable to suppose she would occupy the chief of these. This so-called Mary's room now houses the Wensleydale Folk Museum, a collection of antiquities (assembled in the first place by the late William Horne, of Leyburn). The Folk Museum is under the auspices of the Wensleydale Society, of which Lord Bolton is president.

There are many objects of interest in the museum. The collection of Wensleydale lead-mining tools is said to be one of the finest in the country. Another case displays the original lock from the Castle gatehouse, and there is a piece of plaster moulding which shows the arms of the first Lord Scrope quartered with those of Robert, Lord Tiptoft, whose three daughters and co-heiresses were married to the three sons of Lord Scrope.

The room in the south-west tower (the so-called "Mary's Room") was probably used as an annexe to the Chapel, which opens out of the east door of the room. At the west end of the room is the staircase leading to upper rooms and the roof of the tower. The fireplace is on the north side. On the right-hand side is a recess, nine inches square, running back into the wall and turning at right angles into the flue. Its purpose is vague, though it has been suggested that it was a dry receptacle for tinder.

On the left-hand side of the fireplace a short stair leads into a small chamber (actually part of the west curtain) which is shown to visitors as Mary's bed-chamber. This again, is very doubtful. Because of its nearness to the Chapel and also because of its privacy, it seems more likely that the room served as a sacristy, the place where vestments and altar vessels were kept when not in use in the Chapel. The original mortar floor has recently been re-laid. The roof, also thought to be original, has oak beams, rafters and boards covered with lead. It is still water-tight.

The Upper Rooms Above "Mary's Room" the tower rises, in two storeys of one room each, clear of the south and west curtains.

The first of these rooms is now used as the museum workshop and not shown to visitors. The top room can be seen but not entered, the floor being unsafe. These rooms were most likely used as bed-chambers. Some idea of their original state can be gathered from details of the Scrope will in which the bed hangings and furnishings are described:—Item, "To Roger" his son, "one bed of embroidered velvet, with 4 sides of arras work, and 4 tapestries of the same colour as the said bed, with linen, namely, one pair of 'reynes' (fine linen sheets made at Reunes, Brittany), with mattresse, blankets and canvas,' and to Stephen, a younger son, "one bed complete with side hangings of red, with poplars and embroidered with the Arms of Scrope, together with one hanging tapestry woven with poplars, and 4 tapestries of red embroidered with the Scrope Arms." And to Lord John of Tibbay, "one bed of red with butterflies embroidered with the Scrope Arms, with canopy, hangings and side curtains."

The Roof and Belfries

Most people make the ascent of the tower for the sake of the view which, on a clear day, is fine and extensive. Designed chiefly to serve as a watch-tower it also carried two belfries. The bells, of course, have long since disappeared, but the turrets which housed them remain more or less intact. The one on the south-east corner served the Chapel, and in the remains of the stonework can be seen

Chapel, showing Belfries on South-West Tower

the grooves into which were fitted the supporting timbers ot the bell. At some time since the Castle's dismantling a rude chimney stack of plundered stones has been constructed inside the structure of the turret.

The other bell-turret is built diagonally across the north-east corner of the tower and represents today, as formerly, the crowning feature of the building. Originally it had four trefoil-headed openings. The bell was rung from the courtyard, the rope passing up to and behind the machicolation arch to the roof of the short passage above. Here it entered a square rope-shaft (which can be seen from the gallery in the Chapel) leading direct to the bell turret.

This is the only tower of the building where any of the original battlements remain, and these are only found on the east wall. They do, however, give a good idea of the design of the Castle's defensive system, for originally each tower and all the curtains' walls were provided with battlements. The modern high-pitched roof probably dates from the end of the 18th century. It would replace a practically flat leaded roof.

The West Curtain Like the south-west tower, the west curtain escaped the destroyer's hand in 1647. But not until after the restorations of 1898 could people of modern times see this part in more or less its original state. As far as can be made out the south-west tower, after the departure of the Scrope family at the end

of the 17th century, appears to have served as a farmhouse for the
land now farmed as Castle Bank, which lies south-west of the Castle.
In addition to the farmer's family in the south-west tower, numerous
farm hands, gamekeepers and their families were housed in the west
Curtain, which was partitioned off into a maze-like warren of dwel-
lings and tenements. The East Curtain and remains of the north-east
tower were similarly occupied; a state of affairs not in itself particularly desirable, but one which probably saved the building from
further destruction during the period when castles, abbeys and
churches served as convenient quarries for local building materials.

The Ground   The accommodation contained in this part of the
Floor   building consisted of the armourer's forge (already
                  described in conjunction with the south-west tower),
two stables and a provender house.

The Provender   After passing through the north-west doorway in
House   the courtyard the first door on the left opens into
                     the provender house. Today this is a narrow and
somewhat gloomy chamber with a vaulted roof and three deeply-
arched recesses in the south wall. The first recess opens into the
stables, and the other two towards the west no doubt housed wooden
corn bins. Besoms, shovels and skeps would complete the furnishings.

The   The two vaulted chambers beyond the provender house
Stables   provided accommodation for eight or, at the most, ten
               horses: a number which seems inadequate for times when
the horse was the chief means of transport.

The First   It is unfortunate the visitor is not permitted to enter the
Floor   Castle by the Gatehouse. By entering, as one must today,
                 by the modern door on the west side, the visitor finds
himself immediately in the principal rooms of the building. As these
rooms, for reasons of privacy and security, were placed as far from
the gatehouse as possible, the purpose and importance of the
original entrance is apt to be overlooked.

The Great   A short passage from the west entrance leads into a
Chamber   large well-proportioned room known originally as the
                 Great Chamber. The function of this room, in later
medieval times, was that of a family living room, less formal than
the Great Hall where entertainment was on a grand and ceremonious
scale. Because of its convenient access to the stables and the forge
the Great Chamber no doubt housed equipment and trappings of
the chase as well as the accoutrements of war; all part and parcel
of the everyday medieval scene.
    Prior to the restoration of 1898 this room was carved up into
tenements. There were two or more floors with a maze of small

"Mary's Room"

rooms, staircases and passages which completely hid the fine features of the chamber as seen today. The fireplace, for example, was so built-up with plaster work that its existence was unknown and its discovery a revelation.

The chamber is lit by four windows. The two mullion and transom windows, of six lights each looking into the courtyard, are modern reconstructions of earlier 16th century windows which may have replaced original single-light windows similar to those on the west side of the chamber. Of these latter, the one to the south had its inner rebate and tracery removed to take a doorway at the time when the tenements were constructed. Old photographs of the west curtain showed an exterior stone staircase leading up to this doorway.

A small door in the embrasure of this window opens into a staircase, now broken down, which leads into the armourer's forge. In the north-west corner of the room is a door into what was originally a lavatory, a convenience with which every room in the castle was provided.

The Great Chamber is now adapted as a well-equipped restaurant with a full table licence, an innovation which has proved a great boon to visitors and neighbourhood alike. Hitherto, those who had made a tour of the building, climbing winding stairs and traversing narrow passages—it takes four hours to make a thorough inspection of the castle—were required to travel three or four miles up or down dale before refreshments could be obtained.

The Corridor   A door in the north wall of the restaurant room opens into a wide barrel-vaulted passage with a winding stair at its western end. During the 19th century this passage served as a living kitchen for one of the tenement families, and now, once again, after lying derelict for 60 odd years, it has been converted into a modern kitchen for the preparation of banquets in the

Bolton Castle, once the home of the

Photo: Bertram Unne

Scropes, stands high above Wensleydale

room above. This corridor, however, did not always serve in this menial capacity. During the Castle's heyday it was the chief entry into the Great Hall from the west curtain. Mary of Scotland, when a prisoner here in 1568-69, must have made a daily royal progress along this passage to the banquets and revels in the Great Hall. The door into the Hall was at the east end of the passage, but the entry is now built-up, the Great Hall itself being in ruins. A window has been inserted to light the modern kitchen. The door at the north-east end of the passage opens into a staircase leading down into the stables.

The Upper Room or Solar   The wide staircase at the west end of the passage leads up into the beautiful upper room or solar. (The Solar was a sun room, a feature introduced into many of the later castles in this country). The area of the room takes up practically the whole of the upper floor of the west curtain, and, when the castle was intact, was exceeded in size only by the Great Hall. (The Hall being 51 ft. x 27 ft. and the upper chamber 47 ft. x 24 ft.)

Today the chamber is known as the Banqueting Hall and rightly so, for here, from time to time, are spread many sumptuous meals prepared by the catering concern on the premises. But it was never used for banquets in medieval times, there being neither kitchen nor butteries anywhere in its vicinity, and with such a magnificently arranged Great Hall adjacent to the great kitchen and upper and lower butteries in the north curtain, the idea of a dining room in the west curtain was a superfluity.

The room is lit by two cinque-foil headed windows on the west side, and two six-light mullion and transom windows on the east side looking into the courtyard, and also by a smaller single-light window on the east side. This latter may be one of the original lights, the mullioned windows being 16th Century improvements.

The wide open fireplace is on the west side. At some period during its history the heavy stone lintel has been replaced by the present one, which has a chamfer which does not agree with the original design. In the window embrasure to the right of the fireplace are entrances to lavatories. On the lintel of the north entrance is carved a banker mark in the form of a Roman "T." This sign is found in other parts of the building; in the groined entrance lobby to the Great Hall, and in the bell turrets of the south-west tower, for example.

In the east wall of the alcove in the north-east corner of the room a door opened into a staircase leading to the two upper state rooms of the north-west tower. This was the only entrance to these particular rooms, an arrangement which made them the most private and, at the same time, the most secure rooms in the building. The north-west tower being now in a ruined state, the doorway in the alcove is built up, the staircase behind is said to be still in existence.

The North-West Tower   This tower, like the two already noticed on the south side, is of five storeys, consisting, in this case of a basement and four chambers divided above into two suites of two rooms each. Today the tower is without floors, ceilings and roof, so that what is left of it can be inspected only from the ground floor.

The Basement   Entering by the north-east doorway in the courtyard, the second door on the left leads into the basement. Originally this chamber had a plain barrel-vaulted roof and was lit by two small loopholes on the north side and one on the west (the latter now blocked). In the north-east corner is the entrance to the staircase which ascends, in the thickness of the wall, to the corridor leading to the Hall. In the east wall in as ambry-like recess with the suggestion of a rebate to take a door or doors. The use of this chamber can only be guessed; it may have been a saddle room (in which case the absense of a fireplace is surprising) or it may have been a barn for hay and stable bedding.

The State Chambers   In all castle building of later periods it was the convention to place the state chambers near to the great hall. And so at Bolton we find, as previously stated, two suites of rooms in the north-west tower which is adjacent to the Great Hall in the north curtain. Each room is provided with a fireplace and a lavatory. On the west side of the first, second and third chambers a 16th century mullion and transom window of six lights has been inserted.

The two top chambers were reached by the staircase, already mentioned, which opened from the alcove in the north-east corner of the upper room of the west curtain. This arrangement gave to these chambers a maximum of security and privacy. The lower room of the two has a fireplace which, in its original condition, was more elaborate than any other found in the building. This suggests that it was the most important private room in the Castle.

No doubt it was the room to which Lord Scrope referred in his will as the "Principal chamber" in which were "my bed of embroidered velvet, with four sides of arras work, and four tapestries of the same colour as the said bed, with round bowl and water ewer of silver for the said chamber."

It also seems reasonable to suppose that this room (because of its importance, privacy and security) would be the one allotted to Mary of Scotland during her sojourn here. Although held in "honourable custody" she was allowed to retain her royal status at Bolton, and such a prerogative could, one imagines, command the best chamber.

The lower suite of two rooms (occupying the first and second floors) of this tower was entered from the north-west corner of the Great Hall, where there still exists a lobby connecting the Hall with the first-floor room. From the lobby there is also a staircase (from which the steps were broken at the dismantling) to the room above and a door which opened on to the roof of the north curtain. This staircase did not communicate with the top two rooms of the tower.

The North   The north curtain, like that on the east side, is now in
Curtain   ruins. This state of affairs is due to a succession of
                  misfortunes—firstly, the buffeting of the siege in
1645, followed by the dismantling after the order of 1647—the collapse of the north-east tower in 1761 and the hundred years or so when, without let or hindrance, masonry of the structure was pillaged for building purposes in the surrounding district.

The Ground   The ground floor of the north curtain was divided into
Floor   five vaulted chambers, of which four were connected
                 by a passage running along the south side. The fifth
and most easterly chamber was connected to the north-east tower and entered from the courtyard by a now blocked doorway in the north-east corner. The western chambers were entered by the doorway in the north-west corner of the courtyard, and although this doorway (possibly for reasons of defence) did not differ in design from the other three in the courtyard, it was the chief entrance into the interior of the Castle. Originally it opened into a vaulted passage which ran east for half the length of the curtain and then turned north to the wide stairs which lead into the lobby of the Great Hall.

The Well

Of the two westerly chambers only portions of the dividing walls remain on the north side, but there is sufficient to show that they were barrel vaulted with a door opening into the corridor and a small window in the north wall. They may have been used for stores or stables.

The Wine   In the
Cellar   north wall
                 of the
chamber east of the centre passage there is a winding stair to the buttery above, an arrangement which suggests a wine cellar. The dividing wall between the cellar and the passage is now broken down to ground level, so

that it is difficult to say whether there was a doorway between the passage and the cellar.

The Well The next room is the well Chamber. The well-shaft in
Chamber the south-east corner is said to very deep (it is now partially filled in). Hewn out of the living rock, the well is supposed to be older than the Castle, having served the manor house before the granting of the licence for crenellating in 1378. The top, above the bed of rock, is lined with dressed masonry which, in the form of a semi-circle, is continued to the vaulting of the chamber above. This arrangement enabled water to be drawn up to the butteries and nearby chambers in the kitchen tower.

By means of a splayed stone channel to the right of the well, water could be conveyed to a trough in the courtyard. And by a similar channel (now built up) in the east wall water could be run into the adjoining chamber, which may have been a slaughter house. The job of drawing water, which probably went on all day long, was evidently considered cold enough and wet enough to warrant a fire, there being in the well-chamber one of the only three fireplaces found on the ground floor of the Castle.

The This grim little chamber is situated in the basement of
Dungeon the north turret. It is not, as often stated, completely underground or hewn out of solid rock. The victims were dropped through a square trap in the vaulting to the unpaved floor eight feet below. The heavy flag which sealed the trap and a guard in the small chamber above reduced the chances of escape to nil. Two small comforts were provided—a lavatory and an air-vent. The latter, in addition to providing ventilation, gave sympathetic friends an opportunity to supply prisoners with food and consolation.

The Great The Hall at Bolton occupied the whole of the western
Hall end of the north curtain. It is now in a ruined state, having neither floor nor roof, but in the remaining walls there is sufficient left to give some idea of its former magnificence. As previously stated, the Hall was the largest room in the building, its length being 51 ft. 4 in. and its width 27 ft. 3 in. On each side were three tall cinque-foil headed windows each with transom. Beneath each western window on the north and south sides was a smaller window. These small windows had an importance which might easily pass unnoticed, but their position indicates that this was the "upper" end of the Hall. The "high table" was placed at this end—probably on a dais—and the additional windows were designed not only to throw more light on to the table but to add to the dignity and importance of the people privileged to sit there.

Tall windows on each side were connected with passages which formed gallery-walks. In the heads of the windows can be seen the flues by which smoke escaped from the fire on the central hearth. (It was traditional to retain the central hearth in the halls of castles long after fireplaces had been introduced into other parts of the building). Normally the smoke from these fires escaped via a cupola fitted with louvres in the roof above the fire, but at Bolton these flues were considered a great innovation. Leland during his visit about 1535, noticed them and referred to them in his *Itinerary* as "tunnils" by which "the smoke of the harthe is wonder strangely conveyed."

The North Side of the Great Hall

A first glance at the lower end of the Hall is disappointing, but in the north and south walls can be seen the remains of features from which it is possible to form some idea of the whole. In the north-east corner is the entrance to the lobby which originally had a finely-ribbed vault. This lobby was the chief entrance to the Hall from the courtyard, and it is reasonable to suppose that all distinguished visitors, including of course, Mary of Scotland, would have their first glimpse of the interior of the Castle proper from this lobby. From near the lobby doorway the partition wall between the Hall and the butteries ran from north to south. This wall, called traditionally "the screens", would have two doorways, one for servants to enter by and the other for their exit. Of the two doorways at Bolton only the side of the north door remains. In the south wall can be traced the staircase to the musicians' gallery which conforms to the traditional pattern by being placed above "the screens." Above the musicians' gallery was another chamber, of which nothing remains except the north and south walls—and a fragment of its west wall which has a loop-hole looking down into the Hall.

The loop-hole may be one of several which originally opened from the chamber to the Hall. Their purpose may have been to afford servants or tenants a view of proceedings in the Hall below. Functions in the great halls of castles were usually on a magnificent scale, and those taking part appear to have had no objection to being watched by onlookers, hence the galleries and gallery-walks which were designed to accommodate spectators.

The aspect of the Hall at Bolton today is gloomy and forlorn, but in its original state, with its high roof, tall windows set high up in the north and south walls (which originally were plastered and perhaps decorated), and movable furniture, it must have been both dignified and impressive. Some idea of its former magnificence can be gathered from details of the Scrope will which read as follows:— "For the hall there, my green tapestry woven with griffins with my Arms worked in metal" (probably gold and silver threads). In front of this tapestry would be placed the "high table," probably on a dais, with its linen and plate, also described in the will.

The fact that table linen should be specifically mentioned indicates the extent to which it was valued in the 14th century. It was bequeathed to Richard's two sons, Roger and Stephen, as follows:— "Item, to the said Roger two silver carcatoria and napery for the use of the chief table in the hall of Bolton for continual use, and for six tables (lower tables) in the said hall competent linen for constant covering. Item, to the same Stephen the new napery with long towels always to be used at the principal table, and the new linen napery always to be used at the four other tables of the aforesaid hall, with fine napery and towels for the chief of the aforesaid tables."

The display of gold and silver plate must have been magnificent. It consisted of cups, goblets, plates, dishes, bowls, ewers and, most important of all, salt-cellars. From earliest times salt has been regarded with a reverence which created the symbolic barrier between higher and lower ranks; hence the expression "below the salt." In the will no less than thirty-five salt-cellars are mentioned. Roger being the eldest, surviving son, inherited "one gold salt-cellar with cover, one with lid of silver inscribed with the Arms of the Lord Neville," and in addition he got "12 silver salt-cellars." Stephen got "one salt-cellar with cover, and 12 silver salt-cellars,. Lord John of Tibbay got "six salt-cellars of silver," and in another section of the will "One salt-cellar of silver and 14 silver cups." Bequests to female relatives appear to have been the exception rather than the rule:— To his daughter-in-law, he left *one* salt-cellar in the following affectionate terms:— "to Isabella, my dearest daughter, one salt-cellar." (Isabella was one of the three sisters and co-heiresses, whose fortunes, by their marriage to Lord Scrope's three sons, built up so considerably the prosperity of the Scrope estates!)

Other bequests, to name only a few, were made in the following terms:—"to Lord John of Tibbay, one goblet inscribed with my Arms and the Arms of the Lord Brian of Stapleton;" "to Thomas of Ellerbeck, one silver cup with cover"; "to John of Greneland, one silver cup with a certain superscription engraved upon it." To his

Ground Floor, South-West Tower

son Roger again was left "one round bowl of silver, twelve silver plates, two silver jugs for the upper buttery, one paton with ewer which 'I had as a gift from the Earl of Arundell'."

And so the will continues for many pages. Its chief interest today lies in the light it throws on to a scene of which, as far as the Hall is concerned, only three bare walls remain: gloomy and forlorn indeed, but they are the *actual walls*. The one to the west was the most important. It is green with lichen now, but in its heyday it was hung with the "green tapistry woven with griffins." In the summer of 1568 this tapestry was superseded by another bearing the Arms of Queen Mary of Scotland who, while held in "honourable custody" here was allowed to "put up her cloth of State in the Hall at Bolton." A cloth of state was a ceremonial tapestry hung behind the High Table to denote the rank and importance of those concerned.

The Butteries   East of the Hall in the north curtain were the butteries, of which again nothing remains but the north and south walls. We can, however, assess the size and number of the chambers between the Hall and the Great Kitchen in the north-east tower. The fact that *two* butteries can still be traced is an interesting point, because it tallies with the item in the will, already referred to, "two silver jugs for the upper buttery." Another reference in the will to the buttery is the item "I leave to William of the buttery 10 marks."

Remains of the North-East Tower

The North-East Tower   It is recorded that this tower collapsed and fell without warning on the night of the 19th of November, 1761. Various reasons have been suggested as the cause of the disaster, the chief being the bombardment during the seige of 1645 in which this tower is said to have taken the brunt. Another theory is that the fall was due to the inadequacy of the foundations which were those of the original manor house and, therefore, not designed to carry the weight of a four or five storeyed tower.

There is something to be said for the latter theory, for a glance at the ground plan of the Castle shows the length of this tower to run north and south, whereas in the three other towers the length runs north and west. From this disparity, for which there is no other logical explanation, it has been suggested that the original manor house occupied a position here; the building having an easterly aspect looking down what is now the village of Castle Bolton.

There seems little doubt that the north-east tower is the one referred to in the building contract as the "tower for a kitchen." Of its form and layout nothing now remains except the foundations, and these are confused and misleading as a result of the cottage, now ruined, which was built in their midst during the latter part of the 18th century. The present exterior wall is modern—built of original stones and following the line of the old wall—and was erected to give privacy to the interior parts of the building.

The Great Kitchen would occupy the first floor and thus be in direct communication with the butteries and the Hall.

Of the once busy scene in the Great Kitchen we have an echo in the Scrope will, in which appears the following:— "I leave to Thomas, cook, and to Thomas of the kitchen to each of them 100s." and "To John Payn, John of the bakehouse, and to William of the chamber, to each of them 40s.": "Item: I leave to every page-boy who is in the kitchen at my death, 3s. 4d."

The East Curtain   The state of confusion that exists in the East Curtain today is occasioned, in the first instance, by the fall of the north-east tower and. later, by the erection of tenements amidst its riuns. The tenements themselves are now derelict, so that those who seek to make a reconstruction of this part of the building must sort things out amongst the two sets of ruins. Of the original structure practically only the east and west walls remain, and these show that the range had a separate entrance, defended by a portcullis, from the courtyard. Just inside this entrance a winding stair ascended to the upper chambers: these were the rooms described in the building contract as "between the kitchen-tower and the gatehouse a building . . . having above the vault three rooms one above another."

The Castle from the South

3 - Points of History

T HE Castle was completed in 1399. The same year the Earl of
Wiltshire, son and heir to Richard, First Lord Scrope, was
beheaded at Bristol. Richard died in May, 1403, at the age of seventy-
six. His son, Roger, died in December of the same year.

John Leland, King's Antiquary (Henry VIII) visited Bolton
Castle some time during the 1530s. The entries made in his *Itinerary*
throw much light on the Castle's early history.

In February, 1537, Adam Sedbar, Abbot of Jervaulx, sought
sanctuary in the Castle when his abbey was threatened during the
rising of the Pilgrimage of Grace.

Mary, Queen of Scots, was held in "honourable custody" here
after her defeat at Langside in May, 1568. She arrived at Bolton
one hour after sundown on the 15th of July, 1568. She was moved
from Bolton to Tutbury in January of the following year. Leaving
the Castle on the 26th, she travelled via Ripon where she stayed
overnight. Of the eight or nine castles in which Mary was imprisoned
during the next eighteen years of her life, only Bolton remains.

After the defeat of the King's Army at Marston Moor in 1644,
Bolton Castle was held for the King by John Scrope, natural son of
Emmanuel, eleventh Baron Scrope. The siege lasted more than a

year before the garrison surrendered on 5th November, 1645. John Scrope was fined £7,000 (March, 1646), but before the fine was paid he died in London at the early age of twenty.

In 1647 the Commonwealth Committee at York ordered the Castle to be "rendered untenable."

Richard, the first Lord Scrope, founder of Bolton Castle, was a great patron of the church. At his own request he was buried in the Abbey of St. Agatha, near Richmond. During his lifetime he made many bequests to this religious house, with special reference to the refectory. The Abbey church is now in riuns, the refectory laid low and of his tomb not a trace is to be found. But in his castle, so long as it remains standing at Bolton, Richard will never lack a memorial or testimony to his greatness.

The Gatehouse

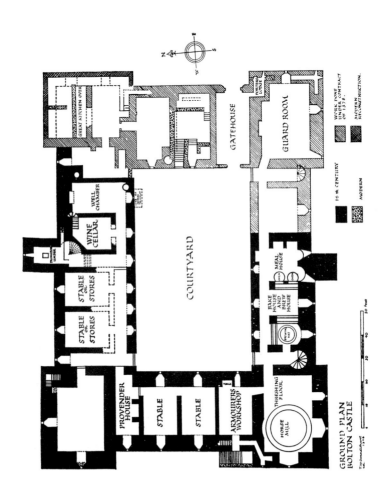

GROUND PLAN
BOLTON CASTLE

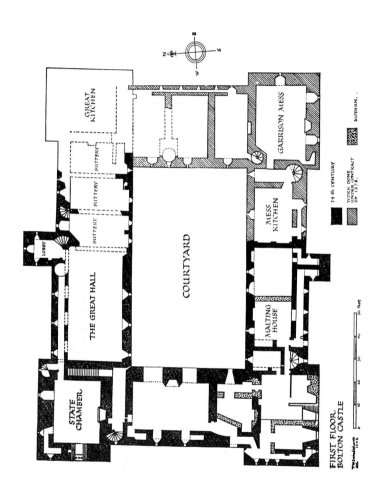

FIRST FLOOR,
BOLTON CASTLE

14 th CENTURY

WORK DONE
UNDER CONTRACT
OF 1378

MODERN.

GREAT KITCHEN

BUTTERY

LOBBY

THE GREAT HALL

STATE CHAMBER

COURTYARD

GARRISON MESS

MESS KITCHEN

MALTING HOUSE

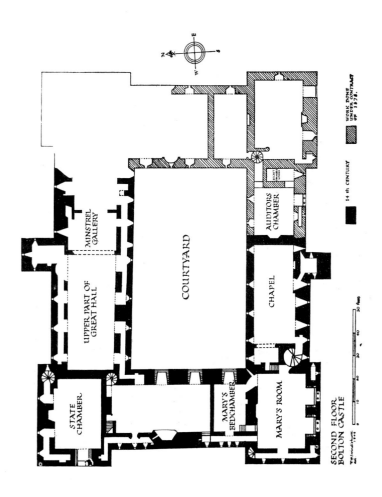

SECOND FLOOR
BOLTON CASTLE